Spatializing Social Justice

Spatializing Social Justice

Literary Critiques

Maryann P. DiEdwardo

Hamilton Books

Lanham • Boulder • New York • Toronto • London

Published by Hamilton Books
An imprint of The Rowman & Littlefield Publishing Group, Inc.
4501 Forbes Boulevard, Suite 200, Lanham, Maryland 20706
Hamilton Books Acquisitions Department (301) 459-3366

6 Tinworth Street, London SE11 5AL

British Library Cataloguing in Publication Information Available

Library of Congress Control Number: 2019930408

ISBN 978-0-7618-7110-1 (pbk. : alk. paper)
ISBN 978-0-7618-7111-8 (electronic)

∞™ The paper used in this publication meets the minimum requirements of American National Standard for Information Sciences Permanence of Paper for Printed Library Materials, ANSI/NISO Z39.48-1992.

Printed in the United States of America

Table of Contents

Acknowledgments

For my editor, Beth Mansbridge, I am so very grateful. Thank you for patience, persistence, and professionalism. I am so blessed to have you as my editor!

I am grateful to, and inspired by, my son Joseph A. DiEdwardo. I prevailed upon him to critique early drafts of the manuscript. He is insightful, thoughtful, and encouraging. Our discussions gave me inspiration to write. His conceptual design drafts for the cover were inspirational as well.

Thanks, as always, to my dear husband Amedeo and my sister Patti, for their support and friendship.

Introduction

This book explores aesthetic cultural landscapes of both physical space and imaginative space. By applying critical hermeneutics and deconstruction, we explore writing and writers. Spatializing social justice reflects on the study of literature, and the notion of space centers on a remembrance of places or settings in fiction. Space is the study of diversity, understanding global perspective, and cultural awareness of diverse peoples through analytical strategies, close reading, the analysis of figurative language, and the comprehension of narrative structure. As such, spatialization as a theoretical model applies a literary spatialization to important works by key authors. The conceptual frameworks of the metaphysics of presence (deconstruction) and metaethics (ethos) seek to resolve questions of human morality by defining concepts such as good and evil, virtue and vice, and justice and crime, by evaluating settings or localities in literature. Examining cultural landscape in literary works relies on research studies in conceptual metaphor theory. Spatialization as a theoretical model applies literary critiques and presents reflections on works by Willa

Cather, Ernest Cline, Zora Neale Hurston, Nella Larsen, Flannery O'Connor, Toni Morrison, and Stephanie Powell Watts.

I

Spatializing Social Justice

Chapter One

Willa Cather

The Space of Landscape in Fiction

CRITICAL HERMENEUTICS

This researcher applies cultural landscape—place that mirrors the functionality of the language of metaphor of imaginary places. Modern literature and critical theory, particularly psychoanalysis, trauma theory, and, most recently, critical human rights and refugee studies are the significant background studies for spatializing imaginary space in texts.

Willa Cather offers us a vision of a narrative space and the trauma of interior personal space in order to share the pain of the main character in *My Mortal Enemy*. Ethos (metaethics) stylistically represents intrapersonal space in the context of Myra's last sentence, "Why must I die like this alone with my mortal enemy!"[1] in Part VII of the book, which was published in 1926, envisions a narrative space. The final words of Cather's main character, who dies alone, claim that she is her own enemy. Death becomes the condition or quality that is transferred with aesthetic action and nature. We find the words of Cather as the signifier of the message of hopelessness. Spatializing the narrative language of Cather reveals her purpose.

Applicable to the study of Cather, the writing about themes of oneself represents our search for interior space. Based on the study of Aristotle's *Poetics* (a free online text and a good companion work to interpret art as imitation), I argue that Cather applies human rights as a methodology to capture and apply the human rights of selfhood in creating works of fiction. First, significant in Cather's message is the suffering in her book, *My Mortal Enemy*. My readings signify Cather as a writer who designs human rights as the cause of the work. Personal voice and female selfhood are components of her work. Recent research in the area of stylometrics explores the ways in which the voice Cather used in her correspondence differs from the voice she used in her public writing. Willa Cather is remembered for her depiction of pioneer life in Nebraska. She established a reputation for giving breadth to the landscapes of her fiction.

Her writing is important to us today in that she is a supporter of human rights. For instance, *Speaking Aloud at Grace Church* was written and compiled by Charles A. Peek, an Episcopal priest and member of the Willa Cather Foundation's Board of Governors. The book is devoted to homilies that Reverend Peek gave at Grace Church in Red Cloud over the two decades spanning the turn of the twentieth to the twenty-first century. The Most Rev. Frank Griswold, former Presiding Bishop of the Episcopal Church, notes: "With great skill and insight, he brings into sharp relief aspects of Cather's personal history and writing which can only deepen and expand our appreciation of what makes her novels and stories timeless in their capacity to reveal truth and the inner working of the human spirit in both its frailty and strength."[2]

NOTES

1. Willa Cather, *My Mortal Enemy, Project Gutenberg Australia*, Part VII, accessed October 30, 2018, http://gutenberg.net.au/ebooks05/0500321h.html
2. Charles A. Peek, The Willa Cather Foundation, *Speaking Aloud at Grace Church*, assessed September 1, 2018, https://www.willacather.org/speaking-aloud-grace-church.

Chapter Two

Toni Morrison

The Space of Modernism

CRITICAL RACE THEORY

In *The Bluest Eye*, Toni Morrison, a modernist, spatializes gender status. The reality of the lack of power of women in history is forever thrust upon us as we read Morrison's *Beloved*, a signifier of the importance of the spiritual in writing and language. In fact, Morrison creates the voice of a dead child to represent spirituality through myth. Baby Sugg's room becomes an island place of worship. Writing is a personal journey determined by the author.

Further, we find in the writing of Kokahvah Zauditu-Selassie, specifically in her book titled *African Spiritual Traditions in the Novels of Toni Morrison*, a support to the use of complexity and metanarratives in episodic installments[1] which are useful to understanding the intricate portrait of self. Perhaps in *Beloved,* the events and circumstances build upon the events to construct dramatic and often heroic portraits of the outcast.

Morrison is one of the most important writers in the modernist period; she is a postcolonial writer. Morrison crafts "theology of narrative,"[2] as Conner points out in his chapter, "Modernity and the Homeless, Toni Morrison and Fictions of Modernism," in the 2014 book, *Toni Morrison: Memory and Meaning*, edited by Adrienne Lanier Seward and Justine Tally, published by University of Mississippi Press, August 2014. Moreover, central to the study of modernism are the collected works of Toni Morrison. Her books form the path for understanding the deeply inherent pain of the exile. Modernism means that period of the early twentieth century connected to the First World War.

NOTES

1. K. Zauditu-Selassie, *African Spiritual Traditions in the Novels of Toni Morrison,* Gainsville: University Press of Florida, 2009.
2. Marc C. Conner, "Modernity and the Homeless, Toni Morrison and the Fictions of Modernism," Part I., *Toni Morison: Memory and Meaning* University of Mississippi Press, 2014.

Chapter Three

Zora Neale Hurston

The Space of Haiti

POETIC PRAXIS, SOUND, SPACE, AND LANGUAGE

Through study of the novels, short stories, essays, and folklore of Zora Neale Hurston, we intend to design a book that relates Hurston's writing to poetic praxis. We decipher signs in literary texts as a symbolic manipulation of the reader by the writer. The signs of space and language as symbolic and allegorical patterns act as contextual frameworks built into characterization and plot. We identify spirituality in writing. Furthermore, the signs are symbols that cause the viewer to question twenty-first-century themes because we synthesize the canon of Zora Neale Hurston as signification of post humanity, which reveals her works as appropriate for citizens in global cultures.

Hurston reaches our minds and hearts with her writing. Her language creates spaces for us to be our authentic selves. She has two voices: her spiritual self and her ethnographic self. A

Zora Neale Hurston novel is a work of poetic praxis. The central purpose of my study concentrates on the use of space, language, and Haitian folklore in the works of Hurston. Digital Humanities, the Hurston archive, forms the basis of my essential argument that the works of Zora Neale Hurston invite continued research. Semiotic praxis is the primary framework, with exploration of works from Zora Neale Hurston's *The Complete Stories*, as well as her book about fieldwork in Haiti, titled *Tell My Horse*.

Space as a form of literary imagination centers on observation of place as an extraordinary connection between literary studies and cultural studies. Hurston offers us an ethnographic view into the feminine. Language portrays the place, the emotion, and the soulful events.

Evaluation of Hurston's stories brings haunting space through language. We find ourselves as passengers on journeys into the creative process of a great voice in any story by Hurston. She shows us how to be curious about all of life, even the harder parts to understand, such as death and representations of the dead human as a wailing creature, or zombie. It is the curious and the metaphysical, originating from Plato, that comes to us as life reflects the spiritual.

Hurston used her travels to Haiti and Jamaica to create. Hurston writes authentic expressions to define space. Her text is connected to the themes of her writings during the period when she wrote each story. Space serves as mythic representation when the creator of the story uses literary imagination to craft artistically. Stories are openings into the soul. Imaginative literature often uses the spirituality of the author. Hurston certainly used her powerful imaginative language to speak of cultural change. Through my own writing and imagination, I seek to prove that Hurston acts as a mirror into cultural changes necessary for all humanity.

Formal study of Hurston continues for me in subsequent studies that I have presented at the Pennsylvania College English Association Conference in University Park, Pennsylvania, at the Penn State University Pennsylvania College English Association Conference. Through the lens of her research on zombies, I found the work, *Tell My Horse*. I concentrate on a summary of the ethnographic portrayal of Haiti and Jamaica in the book *Tell My Horse*. With the use of firsthand accounts of weird mysteries and the horrors of voodoo, *Tell My Horse* is an invaluable resource and fascinating guide. It is based on Zora Neale Hurston's personal experiences in Haiti and Jamaica, where she participated as an initiate.

The short stories of Zora Neale Hurston break down interior interpersonal borders. Psychological space is the result. By the concentrated study of sets of short stories that contain meaningful themes, characters, and human emotions, readers can significantly conquer self-doubt and break down self-imposed borders. Through reading, analyzing, discussing, and eventually writing short stories, creative writers develop self-understanding.

The most important aspect of the short story as a literary powerhouse remains that reading and writing the genre can elicit personal transformation. We write a few pages of text that reveal understanding of the self. Through interpretation, we learn. By condensing thoughts and writing a shorter version, writers find success. Certainly, the short story as a genre transforms by centering a story upon the self-discovery of the writer, to promote change and personal growth. Furthermore, I use the short story as an authentic assessment to break down borders between the academic desert of literature as a viewed subject, to literature as an experienced, vast space that transforms.

BACKGROUND: ZORA NEALE HURSTON'S FIRST SHORT STORY

Hundreds of writers and artists lived in Harlem in the 1920s and 1930s and were part of a vibrant, creative community that found its voice in what came to be called the Harlem Renaissance. Alain Locke's 1925 collection *The New Negro: Voices of the Harlem Renaissance* —a compilation of literature by and essays about New Negro artists and black culture—became a "manifesto" of the movement. Some of black America's foremost writers contributed stories and poems to the volume. The work of these artists drew on the African American experience and expressed a new pride in black racial identity and heritage. Zora Neale Hurston—novelist, folklorist, and anthropologist—was known during the Harlem Renaissance for her wit, irreverence, and folk-writing style. She won second prize in the 1925 literary contest of the Urban League's journal, *Opportunity*, for her short story "Spunk," which also appeared in *The New Negro*.

Hurston influences Albert Chinualumogu Achebe, born November 30, 1930, who is one of the most significant writers to emerge from contemporary Africa. His literary vision has profoundly influenced the form and content of modern African literature.

The short story "Girls at War," by Chinua Achebe, from the collection of his short stories titled *Girls at War and Other Stories* (New York: Anchor Books, 1972), as well as his important novel *Things Fall Apart*, are the foundation of my introductory writing lessons for students studying composition. I form the discussions by offering the idea that Achebe has created a singular important voice, his own spiritual quest, to revitalize his nation of Nigeria through his literature. To connect cultures—mine and theirs—the literary scholar and twenty-first-century students—we watch the music video by The Roots, called "Things Fall Apart," which was named after Achebe's novel and uses the same themes, with a few changes, to depict the tensions of the clashes of culture in the city. *All Things Fall Apart* will be the title of the newest movie to come from the same themes by 50 Cent, who altered the name. The film was scheduled to open at the Urbanworld Film Festival on September 18, 2012. The singer offered Achebe one million dollars to use the title of the book, but Achebe refused.

We read the following poem, which is the source of the title of Achebe's novel: William Butler Yeats's "The Second Coming" (1921). Yeats was attracted to the spiritual and occult world, and fashioned for himself an elaborate mythology to explain human experience. "The Second Coming," written after the catastrophe of World War I and with communism and fascism rising, is a compelling glimpse of an inhuman world about to be born. Yeats believed that history in part moved in two-thousand-year cycles. The Christian Era, which followed that of the Ancient World, was about to give way to an ominous period represented by the rough, pitiless beast in the poem. Yeats imagines that the great heritage of Western European civilization is collapsing and that the world will be swept by a tide of savagery from the "uncivilized" portions of the globe. As you read the novel, try to understand how Achebe's work is in part an answer to this poem.

Things Fall Apart, published in 1958, is the original African novel in English. Its most striking feature is its creation of a complex and sympathetic portrait of a traditional village culture in Africa. Achebe is trying not only to inform the outside world about Ibo cultural traditions, but to remind his own people of their past and to assert that it had contained much of value. All too many Africans in his time were ready to accept the European judgment that Africa had no history or culture worth considering. The language of the novel is simple yet dignified. When the characters speak, they use an elevated diction. This is meant to convey the sense of Ibo speech. This choice of language was a brilliant and innovative stroke, given that most earlier writers had relegated African characters to pidgin or inarticulate gibberish. One has the sense of listening to another tongue—one with a rich and valuable tradition.

Zora Neale Hurston, who was born in 1891 and died in 1960, has been rediscovered in a manner unprecedented in the black tradition. Several black women writers in America today have openly turned to her works as sources of narrative strategies—to be repeated, imitated, and revised—in acts of textual bonding. Hurston claimed that she wanted to write a black novel and not a treatise on sociology. It is this urge that resonates in Toni Morrison's *Song of Solomon* and *Beloved.*

The short story "Girls at War," by Chinua Achebe, and "Magnolia Flower," by Zora Neale Hurston, both suggest that themes are the first element of literary thought that break down interpersonal borders. Achebe recreates, with energy and authenticity, the major social and political issues that confront a contemporary African on a daily basis. Hurston uses mythic realism, modernism, and imagery of the river and "The Mighty One" to create a thematic world with allegory and myth. These serve as vehicles for the representation of the conflicts and dilemmas that African Americans share with all other human beings (Gates and Lemke, Introduction).

Next, characters in the two short stories, "Girls at War," by Chinua Achebe, and "Magnolia Flower," by Zora Neale Hurston, signify that students need interpersonal knowledge to filter the literature into meaningful attributes that echo their own lives or aspects of their contemporary culture. Gladys, a beautiful girl who has been forced to become a woman (kept by some army officer in her struggle for survival during the war) dies in the last scene, in a dramatic "shattering of sky" in the reality of the Biafran war in Nigeria. Her death forces the reader to see the reality and truth of war. Achebe deals with the themes of African American tradition: from the disintegration of old tribal customs to political turmoil in Nigeria. On the other hand, Hurston creates Magnolia, who experiences the abuse of her father because she fell in love with John. She runs away with her lover, and comes back forty years later.

Zora Neale Hurston may be the creator of one of the first creative nonfiction works about a real-life zombie. In *Tell My Horse*, her 1938 recounting of her fieldwork in Haiti, she talked about what she'd seen.

Archetypes are personified symbols of various human qualities. The zombie is the shadow archetype which is rebellious and out of harmony with the laws of nature. Upon the creation of a zombie archetype, the writer creates a new reflection of the present reality. Masculine and feminine zombie archetypes enliven creative nonfiction writers and poets. As a writer and a teacher of writing, I involve my students in the creative process with the use of zombie themes. By engaging a pop-culture meme, I propose that the zombie acts as meme model, changing the paradigm of writing classes to include students as doers, thinkers, publishers, editors, and concept mappers. As a vital part of twenty-first-century pedagogy, the zombie offers me the chance to reach my students by telescoping into a subgenre of horror with characters who oppose humans who wish to create a most fulfilling life without bringing harm to self or others. The writer's mind grasps the archetype as a mythical figure separate from reality. The zombie archetype is a meme that holds the power, for a time during the plot, to restructure and reenvision death.

However, I am looking for roots in short story writers and poets as well. For the purpose of my study, I also delve into literary research for clues. Furthermore, Haitian folklore (Zonbi) (NPR) and the works of Zora Neale Hurston underlie important elements of the archetype. Both Poe and Hurston modify the zombie archetype as a reflection of their cultures. Poe (Hatter) may be credited with a zombie creation in his short story, "The Fall of the House of Usher."

My references also focus on a new book called *Undead: Revived, Resuscitated, and Reborn*, an intriguing new book from Abingdon Press. It's a book about zombies—a Christian book about the undead. In it, author Clay Morgan explores death and the supernatural, explaining how faith and the living dead intersect. Clay Morgan:

> I wrote a book about zombies for much the same reason C. S. Lewis wrote a book like *The Screwtape Letters*, about demons—to find light in the darkness. Tales of supernatural are ready-made for Christianity. Zombies are ridiculously popular and culturally relevant, so zombies are a

> great way to get someone's attention. From there we can have a marvelous discussion about spiritual life and spiritual death.[1]

AMC's hit show *The Walking Dead* is a model that reflects students' stories of pain in personal lives. Pedagogy based on place memory of the supernatural suggests that reflection, active learning, and publication are the goals. Involve students quickly. Introductions allow identity early in the course protocol; writing and thinking activities promote self-efficacy; to build confidence, invite students to create assignments or other requirements, or act as concept mappers of the class environment. Publishing as a goal creates student writers who are going to value the class and its requirements. Write a novelette exploring zombies and faith.

Alternatively, poetry workshops during writing sessions offer students active learning as well. Do journaling during session, with group presentations. I focus on pedagogy for the poet, which is based on place memory of the supernatural. Reflecting on the process and the designing of life-story projects about a living or deceased person's home or vacation spot act as metacognitive preliminary assignments to teach poetry in zombie meme. Write a short summary of a favorite character's language patterns. Telescope into the dialogue and setting, costume and lighting, and then review all aspects of specific scenes as a way to see ideas in visual form. Mystery is a style, a tone—a set of principles that guides a writer and allows a theme to develop with the writer's voice.

How does the zombie archetype relate to the current cultural milieu? How can students research, write group essays, or develop masculine or feminine archetypes with creative freedom? How can a dialectical journal enhance the class? The answer is to write with the writers whom you are teaching. I gain insight into writing by writing, and teach this theory. Imaginative literature utilizes a reflection of reality. Writers and poets act as visionaries who compress emotions into words. Mythical in theme, zombie archetypes offer visions of experiences beyond the human realm. Zombie archetypes of the masculine and feminine natures reverse roles and create death as a paradigm for healing from the pain of life on earth. Zombie memes tells us that imaginative literature and film reveal cultural patterns. We are a grieving culture. We are a spiritual culture. We are not alone. We can write based on past cultural milieu. We like to use meme to represent ourselves. Meme of the zombie tells us that imaginative literature and film as well as poetry reveal cultural patterns. Zombie archetypes include the following: grieving culture, spiritual culture, saddened culture, gathering of dead ancestors or others, history of myths, and other memes such as photography, comics, dance, music, and art.

The value of any experience derives from reflection. My own mythic adventure into the world of zombie archetypes includes the creation of my own male and female zombie archetypes based on a weird but interesting experience. I incorporate the story in this creative nonfiction essay to emphasize the importance of creating writing by using a spark of the internal mechanism of imagination. Creative nonfiction techniques with emphasis on the author's purpose, a vision of the audience as receptor of the story, and the message help student writers to succeed by allowing them to be dramatists. I read my stories to my students and have never lost my quest to write. My journals are filled with stories based on my encounters with zombie archetypes as ghosts or amazing sightings that, to the ordinary person, would seem insignificant; to me, a writer and a poet, these moments border on the extraordinary or metaphysical. Modern encounters with death may bridge the transformation in the literature classroom from just observer to doer. Authors and publishers may result.

Zombie archetypes may act as historically spiritual foundations. I experienced a zombie story in my own vacation setting the summer of 2014. For me, as a creative nonfiction author, zombie archetype is myth in the form of spiritual awakening. The soul may be the connection between the story, the student, the poem, and the reflection of reality. Harmony may result by the archetypal study of yin, feminine, and yang, masculine. We are now not past and not future. This is the message of the writer.

Imaginative literature reflects reality. Writers and poets act as visionaries who compress emotions into words.

NOTE

1. Clay Morgan, *Undead: Revived, Resuscitated, Reborn* Nashville: Abington Press, 2012.

Chapter Four

Nella Larsen

The Space of the East Village

HARLEM RENAISSANCE

Nellallitea "Nella" Larsen, born Nellie Walker (April 13, 1891–March 30, 1964), was an American novelist of the Harlem Renaissance. Larsen's capacity to describe the psychological effects of the "color line" beyond any "tragic mulatto" stereotype happens to be her most lasting contribution to African American literature[1] (Joseph A. DiEdwardo, unpublished paper). Like a number of African American women writers of the New Negro Renaissance (including Jessie Fauset and Zora Neale Hurston), Larsen never lived to see her novels *Quicksand* (1928) and *Passing* (1929) become part of the canon of African American literature.

When Nella Larsen died in 1964, she was working as a supervisory nurse in the psychiatric ward. Larsen's public career was defined less by pathology and more by her ability to uncover the psychology and pretensions of European America and the African American middle class with whom she has often been identified. As the mixed-race daughter of a working-class Danish American woman and raised in the rough neighborhoods of Chicago, she fit no more "naturally" into African American high society than she did among neighboring whites.

In *Quicksand,* Larsen uses concepts which concern the space of trauma. In chapter one, Larsen writes:

> She loved this tranquility, this quiet, following the fret and strain of the long hours spent among fellow members of a carelessly unkind and gossiping faculty, following the strenuous rigidity of conduct required in this huge educational community of which she was an insignificant part. This was her rest, this intentional isolation for a short while in the evening, this little time in her own attractive room with her own books.[2]

In the textual clues, Helga Crane—the tragic mixed-race protagonist in this novel—thinks:

> He feared and hated her. She pitied and despised them. Uncle Peter was different. In his contemptuous way he was fond of her. Her beautiful, unhappy mother had been his favorite sister. Even so, Helga knew that he would be more likely to help her because her need would strengthen his oft-repeated conviction that because of her Negro blood she would never amount to anything, than from motives of affection or loving memory. This knowledge, in its present aspect of truth, irritated her to an astonishing degree.[3]

We see that Larsen is describing the narrative from a female point of view, which is the ebb of second-wave feminism. *The Wiley Blackwell Anthology of African American*

Literature – Volume 2: 1920 to the Present, First Edition, edited by Gene Andrew Jarrett, is poignant with the presentation of short biographical sketches before important works. For example, in the text we can study a series of authors who represent important historical periods of African American literature. The biographical section about Nella Larsen is quite compelling.

Nella Larsen's *Quicksand* and *Passing* are novels which represent the cultural landscape of signs of loss. I practice searching for praxis within the study of semiotics in my lectures, essays, and books. Praxis is the ability of the writer to achieve a high moment of clarity about the human condition. Praxis joins other signs of cultural change: the literary elements of characterization and plot. The writer then creates multiple fields for readers to use and upon which to base their visit of the fictional work. The creation of the inner life of a character through narrative lies within the substantive study of the semiotic basis for the narrative by Larsen. Creation of narrative eventually demands characterization and other devices such as dialogue and dramatic effect within the creative space in the fictional world. Let us define that creative process and relate to the use of narrative as a semiotic vision. A narrative in the fictional world makes the characters at risk of failure. Nella uses the humanity of her own experiences as the principle of her fictional works.

In the study of the novel and the novel as a narrative, we suggest that Nella Larsen picked up observances of cultural milieu—in her experiences in Harlem, in particular. These led her to some knowledge of the aspects of a natural social phenomenon. The semiautobiographical book *Quicksand,* (my favorite novel), is about Helga, born to a white mother and an absent black father. As a young woman, Helga teaches, as I do. Moving to Harlem and eventually to Denmark, she attempts a new life.

Nella Larsen's novel, *Passing*, is centered on the narrative by a fictional character, Clare Kendry, a light-skinned biracial woman living as a white woman. In its way, this novel breaks down the thematic binary of black and white with its depiction of racial passing. In addition to the sign of a binary of black and white, Larsen's novel simultaneously explores the theme of gender.

The historical, cultural, and literary functions of the novel amount to a genre of change. As we focus on *Quicksand* and *Passing*, we study recurring forms and techniques of the form as narrative and a dominant literary social document. Projects that we teach students based on the writing of Nella may become a novella or a book chapter with an awareness of responsibilities to create a novel. With a class based on the creative narrative of Nella Larsen, we emphasize the study of diversity, understanding global perspective, cultural awareness of diverse peoples through analytical strategies, close reading, the analysis of figurative language, and the comprehension of narrative structure.

Historically, we continue to see that Zora Neale Hurston was influenced in the twentieth century by Nella Larsen. Both authors show us how to write about real events in order to make a difference. The spatializing of Nella Larsen also includes the nature of the educational community as viewed through feminist theory, to reveal Nella Larsen as imperative for 21st-century literary scholarship, in the same capacity as we include Langston Hughes. She offers us methodology and pedagogical structure which allows writers to explore the period of the Harlem Renaissance within the themes of post feminism and the many ways in which women are often fearful, subject to rape and other kinds of violence. In her writing, Nella Larsen also examines the politically and economically underprivileged.

NOTES

1. Joseph A. DiEdwardo, "Unpublished Paper on Nella Larsen". Contributor to *American WomenWriters, Poetics, and the Nature of Gender Study,* Ed. Maryann P. DiEdwardo. Cambridge
Scholars Publishing, 2016.
2. Nella Larsen, *Quicksand, First Start Publishing eBook,* edition October, 2012.
3. Nella Larsen, *Quicksand.*

Chapter Five

Flannery O'Connor

The Space of the South

DECONSTRUCTION

We learn the opposite of peace in the works of Flannery O'Connor. Readers feel despair. She combines the Tao and the Christian theologies. O'Connor was born in Savannah, Georgia, in 1925. A devoted Catholic, she lived most of her life on a farm. She wrote two novels and thirty-two short stories, reviews, and commentaries. Her Southern Gothic style uses regional settings and grotesque characters. Long after her 1964 death, her compiled writings won the 1972 U.S. National Book Award for Fiction. Catholic revival and a Catholic theory of fiction, as well as Christian realism of the here and now and postwar America, are themes that highlight our quest for understanding of O'Connor's writing found in her private journal titled *A Prayer Journal*.

A Prayer Journal was published in 2013 by Farrar, Straus and Giroux, New York, USA. As soon as I realized that the private journaling of one of my favorite authors was available, I purchased and read the book. Observing the prayers of O'Connor defines the poetics of her inner life. The book changed me.

We find the tumultuous South represented in O'Connor. During the twentieth century, the space of the South is essential to her purpose. She lived during the civil rights movement. Therefore she uses the reversal of human rights in her stories. Characters are sullen and dark. Yet, in *A Prayer Journal*, O'Connor writes with language that is written for God alone. A Christian, she uses beautiful intrapersonal expression. The book has both dated and undated entries. For instance, I appreciate those pages which show her handwritten entries. The poetics of O'Connor are based on her writings to the Lord. We recognize her journaling as a daily writing practice paramount to the writer's ethic. The powerful language and poetics of the works by Flannery O'Connor will change us as we experience her inner life. Therefore, an analysis through the lens of the definition of civil rights portrays Flannery O'Connor as a leader in the thematic approach to ethics and human dignity. She wrote about the human condition with a poetic voice that mattered, which also applies to our times in the twenthy-first century.

Thomas Merton's prose elegy honors the late writer Flannery O'Connor, in *Raids on the Unspeakable*, his 1966 collection of contemplative essays. Intertextuality is the point of the structure and the significance of Merton's thoughts in his elegy. Merton points out that Flannery O'Connor respected her characters by writing truth. Often, these thoughts can take the form of metaphor. One message in the form of words can really mean another message. Historically, the elegy matters to us since it is a document that is retained in the archives of Thomas Merton. Available to researchers for study, the document first appeared to be published in 1964 in the bound volume, *Merton, Collected Essays*. The work is the third essay in his book of collected essays titled, *Raids on the Unspeakable*.

Culturally, the elegy signifies the importance of the intersection of literature and religious imaginative writing. The ultimate spiritual vacuum of the unspeakable is where violence can enter. Arguably, in the twenty-first century we are bound by metaethics. Meta-ethical positions may be divided according to how they respond to questions such as in protected settings, so that the dialogue is private to that particular day and time only. O'Connor writes about the darkness of life. The publication of her journal was significant. We have the words of truth that she wrote to herself. Perhaps the journal is a sign that the author wrote fiction to hide her own sorrows. If illness is a visionary state, then Flannery O'Connor was a visionary of significance.

Chapter Six

Ernest Cline

The Space of Posthumanity

SEMIOTIC PRAXIS

Architectural structures materialize posthumanity in *Ready Player One*, the 2011 novel by Ernest Cline. Architecture in this book is a sign of dystopian functionality, a connectivity to redefine posthuman, and a revelation of the disintegrating social order. The dystopian functionality that Cline manipulates within the crumbling space where his characters dwell is a new earth, a virtual world, where the planet shows the deterioration that Cline has frosted with the results of global warming. Cline's vision may be extrapolated from other science fiction authors, one of them being Margaret Atwood.

My argument concentrates on architecture, or place, for use as one of the signs of a dystopian future. The unity of place and plot faces us as a device to offer a way to step out of our own universe and into the weird world of the future. Semiotic praxis creates multiple fields for readers to use, to base our visit in the fictional work. Dystopian places breed self-doubt. The creation of the place in the book uses dystopian architecture. The purpose of the author is the key to understanding the importance of space and place in literary works. Vital to the creative process, the author crafts a visual representation. We see the place and space in the book via description of place where Wade lives on a dying planet; the idea represents a dystopian future. The visual form, the space and the place, is a sign. Therefore, we learn more about our future on earth through Cline's setting. His characters move with trepidation within the digital and real worlds. Creation of place eventually demands characterization and other devices such as dialogue and dramatic effect within the dystopian world. Let us define that creative process and relate it to the use of both literature and architecture as a semiotic vision. A dysfunctional community in a dystopian world makes the characters at risk of failure. Fear is a predominant theme. The character Art3mis is a great example of semiotic praxis within a dystopian universe.

Dystopian functionality in *Ready Player One* finds a basis in the concept of semiotics—the general science of signs—which clearly embodies Cline's methods in his creation of *Ready Player One*. We argue that Cline's work functions as a sign, connects us to our futures, and changes social order to include posthumans. Characters live in dystopian spaces which halt human emotions. Nick Bostrom, from the Future of Humanity Institute, Oxford University, writes an article about posthuman qualities. Extreme human enhancement could result in "posthuman" modes of being. After offering some definitions and conceptual clarification, I argue for two theses. First, some posthuman modes of being would be worthwhile.

Second, it could be good for human beings to become posthuman.

Ready Player One, Part Two. Semiotic praxis yields a lens into the brilliant new book and the film based on it which premiered on March 11, 2018. Insights into the book *Ready Player One* decidedly use signs to predict drastic cultural change. We become virtual in the book. The dystopian work is an allegory. God is not present in the psyche of the main character. The novel is set in a not-too-distant future where advanced internet, gaming, and virtual reality technologies have changed the world as we know it, and led to the creation of the OASIS, a virtual reality universe that people live in and value more than the real world.

Cline's use of societal dysfunctionality—reflecting our current socioeconomic virtual dependency—is a sign that creates mythic connectivity. We experience a dystopia. In *Ready Player One*, the author points to a time in the future when unbridled corporate greed creates an alternate condition. Wade, the main character, lives in an old trailer stacked on top of other rotting trailers. Cline uses creation of imagined dystopian architecture to expose that the OASIS ceased to be an open-sourced, virtual utopia. His vision is a reflection of his interpretation of our current global economic crisis. Cline crafts social order to comment on twenty-first-century greed and economic crisis as well. A biomimetic look at the book shows loss of the natural world in the genre, as well as an extrapolation of a darker vision of our future. He projects an imagined future based on the pop culture of the past. He alludes to film, literature, and gaming themes to enhance his work.

In 2006, Nick Bostrom defined posthuman as a being who owns a social order that, among other things, manifests "cognition—general intellectual capacities, such as memory, deductive and analogical reasoning, and attention, as well as special faculties such as the capacity to understand and appreciate music, humor, eroticism, narration . . ."[1] such as we find in Cline's main characters. Ultimately, dystopian creation is important to the meaning of the work; dystopian visions symbolize the representation of a place symbolic of posthumanity.

The aesthetic functionality of dystopian structures within the elements of literature builds pathos in the dystopian novel and relies on dystopian-framed visual context as semiotic praxis. Furthermore, contextualization depends on architecture as an element of the aesthetic creative process. Cline's adventure uses imagined architecture as a lens. Architecture materializes through grammatical structures to create ideologies of social hierarchy. Applying space and place to an alarmingly unpleasant world, Cline extrapolates to project the future. His dystopian creation works as an opportunity to add significantly to the emotional appeal of the work. Dystopian architecture in the allegory symbolizes representation of place as mythic creation.

NOTE

1. Nick Bostrom, "Why I Want to Be a Posthuman When I Grow Up" eds. Bert Gordijn and Ruth Chadwick, *Medical Enhancement and Posthumanity* (Oxford University: Future of Humanity Institute, 2008) 107–137.

Chapter Seven

Stephanie Powell Watts

Space and the Short Story

JOURNALING THE STREETS OF THE PAST TO UNDERSTAND LITERARY WORKS

Stories based on real experiences by talented authors provide material for fascination and literary critiques. Stephanie Powell Watts is an American author. She won a Whiting Award in 2013 and an Ernest J. Gaines Award for Literary Excellence in 2012 for her book, *We Are Taking Only What We Need*, eleven stories comprising a collection which chronicles the lives of African Americans in North Carolina.

Message, meaning, community, and conceptual theory in "Unassigned Territory", a literary critique, analyzes the story to emphasize the importance of its contribution to literature. In fact, Stephanie Powell Watts was recognized by The Pushcart Prize: Best of the Small Presses series, published every year since 1976, a literary project in the United States. Dr. Powell Watts also shares in two volumes of Best New Stories from the South anthologies, as well as praise by *Oxford American*, *New Letters*, *African American Review*, and elsewhere. She has received the *Atlantic Monthly* nonfiction prize. In her first book of short stories, she wrote "Unassigned Territory," a highly developed model for the short story.

In "Unassigned Territory," Watts invites us with message to be and to read with empathy. As Watts pulls us into the space of North Carolina, we are drawn into the meaning and imagery of heat as we sit with the characters in an old car; we are placed into the metaphor by the author's skill at using heat "hot enough to fry eggs" so that we are weary on the first page. Concepts of tone, style, and action fill us with vulnerability, not hope. We are reminded of sweltering days when we may have been younger and less savvy to the dangers of heat and interiors of cars. By page two, we learn that the author, who is very present in the space of the story, uses the name Steph. Through space and community, Stephanie Powell Watts develops a narrative of compelling strength, rich with metaphors of spatial importance to the meaning of community. The narrative space is interior and intrapersonal for the main character and yet expands to show us the small community. At the end of the story, the narrator admits to us that she may love a community member, a woman named Phyllis. Then, the narrator wonders about the nature of love. Action, interior monologue, and interior spaces are essential to the story and to the conceptual theoretical spaces within the writing. We are allowed to visualize the mind of the narrator, and the stories within the mind of the narrator create a new place, a private place, for only the narrator and the reader secretly to experience.

Conceptual mindfulness and the voice of the narrator function as meaning, message, and concept of space, and as metaphor and truth. Our fascination with the short story dwells on the use of place to represent community, as metaphor for creativity in a short work of fiction. We may be able to signify that the most important contribution of Stephanie Powell Watts is literary truth. Her elements of design are woven into a space of dramatic wonder. Stream of consciousness with questions about love and faith shock us. Interior monologues are spaces of freedom. Watts uses these spaces to achieve high art within her short story.

II

Reflections

Chapter Eight

Reflection on Chapter 1, Willa Cather

We become agents of change if we share the discoveries that research and reading offer us. We can take action and go further than our heroes.

Reflection on the study of literature and space was based on a remembrance of a marvelous day of writing. The basic formula includes the wisdom of Plato's *Phaedo* as a backdrop to my own efforts to write. Also, my own thoughts on literacy apply to my self-knowledge of mechanisms that form my writing goals. Primarily, I am a teacher and a speaker. To present wisely, I create short and long presentations. The days that I write hold opportunities for self-growth. I not only grow as a writer, but I also grow as a human being and an artist of words. Essentially, I claim that writing is a human right.

My day begins at 4:00 a.m. I read several texts. From writing, I have found a renewed sense of self that has resolved fears previously created in my own mind about the whole process of writing. Indeed, the concentration embedded within my single important task of sharing with others has changed the trajectory of my day of writing. I am also journaling about that marvelous writing day which seemed to be an epiphany day. Literacy also includes the abilities to access knowledge through technology and to search for complex texts. Literacy is the lifelong intellectual process of gaining meaning from a critical interpretation of written or printed text. The blending of previous learning with new skills will enhance study. I suggest that we add reading and writing in capacities that we may not even realize yet, such as audio and real-life events. I argue that Willa Cather applies human rights as a methodology.

The Willa Cather Archive features pages such as Rediscovering Serena's Album. In February 1887, Serena White of Nuckolls County, Nebraska, received a friendship album titled Mental Portraits, probably as a sixteenth birthday gift. These books, also known as autograph albums or confession albums, were enduringly popular in the late nineteenth century, usually purchased in stationery stores rather than bookstores, and widely given as gifts to women and girls. Serena's album has long been an object of curiosity because one of its more colorful entries was made by a precocious fourteen-year-old.

An entry by Serena's classmate, Willa Cather, was first published in 1951 in *The World of Willa Cather*, by Mildred Bennett, founder of the Willa Cather Foundation. For its fascinating look at the writer in her adolescence—and her world—Serena's album is a treasure.

Chapter Nine

Reflection on Chapter 2, Toni Morrison

My research presents literary critiques focused on the imagined cultural landscape of specific literary works and associated activities such as fine art, music, poetry, digital humanities, and primary source activities that the author promotes to gain radical compassion. Further, this researcher advocates evidence-based change through service writing, volunteering at local and regional as well as national community engagement events to inspire civic values.

We connect luminaries such as Dietrich Bonhoeffer, Flannery O'Connor, Thomas Merton, and Martin Luther King Jr. through critical hermeneutics. "That is the secret of art, and of its effect upon us. The creative process, so far as we are able to follow it at all, consists in the unconscious activation of an archetypal image, and in elaborating and shaping this image into the finished work. By giving it shape, the artist translates it into the language of the present, and so makes it possible for us to find our way back to deepest springs of life. Therein lies the social significance of art; it is constantly at work educating the spirit of the age, conjuring up the forms in which the age is most lacking."[1]

Spatializing and reimagining writing for the purpose of peace shares Dr. Maryann DiEdwardo's newest research, which involves identifying key images, values, beliefs, and social structures that point toward a particular cultural movement. She explains her own healing and transformative experiences based on her reading of the works of Nella Larsen, Willa Cather, Toni Morrison, and Flannery O'Connor, to signify that the themes of trauma have a lasting effect. Maryann studies letters and archival evidence to acknowledge space as a methodology to teach peace. In fact, the study of peace defines the human experience.

Maryann P. DiEdwardo is the author of more than forty books and articles, including "Pairing Linguistic and Music Intelligences." Her case study research connects music as representative of culture and relates to the rhetoric found in literary passages. For modern readers, what a work of fiction "really means" is the subject of endless, conflicting interpretations. "The first task of literary criticism is precisely this: to translate into ideas the image of the world that lies sedimented inside the works. And yet this happens with the awareness that the language of mimesis possesses a truth that is irreducible to the medium of the concept."[2]

NOTES

1. Carl Yung, *The Portable Yung,* Hull, R.F.C. trans., edited by Campbell, Joseph, New York: Penguin Books, 1971.
2. Guido Mazzoni, *Theory of the Novel* Harvard University Press. iBooks https://itunes.apple.com/us/book/theory-of-the-novel/id1190351004?mt=11

Chapter Ten

Reflection on Chapter 3, Zora Neale Hurston

My writing in the area of semiotics and intertextuality continues regarding the cultural poetics of Zora Neale Hurston. The short story "Black Death," which predates second-wave feminism, is a prelude to Hurston's Haitian folklore: *Mules and Men* (1935) and *Tell My Horse* (1938). She was writing about cultural contextual clues in order to decipher clues about multiple strands of complexity. Imaginative literature often uses the spirituality of the author. Hurston certainly used her powerful imaginative language to speak of cultural change.

Through my own writing and imagination, I seek to prove that concentration on the art of writing is a mirror into cultural changes that are necessary for all humanity. Cultural poetics tries to identify key images to identify literature as a social text or discourse. Through the lens of cultural poetics and semiotics, in a new book (with a 2018 date of publication), we signify Hurston's identity as a "literary anthropologist" and her thematic messages rooted in folklore are based in expressions of space and language.

I have been researching her works since 1977. I have presented papers on Zora Neale Hurston for International Conferences since 2007. I have used her works to teach Freshman English at three major universities: Penn State University Lehigh Valley campus, during a writing classes in 2006; University of Maryland University College, online classes from 2010 to the present; and Lehigh University, from 2007 to the present. I used the works of Zora Neale Hurston, based on her studies in Haiti, to teach civil rights ideas at the Northampton Community College (2003 to 2007) and Lehigh Carbon Community College (2005–2007). I am editor and contributor to a text (in 2016 with Cambridge Scholars Publishing) based on a panel that I designed for the Northeast Modern Language Association. I have been a teacher of an African American literature course at the University of Maryland University College, as well.

My study of the works of Hurston is rooted in my determination to gather support for her writings. Hurston was born on January 7, 1891, in Notasulga, Alabama, and died on January 28, 1960, in Fort Pierce, Florida. In the essay, "Characteristics of Negro Expression" (1934), she describes her rich and flexible uses of folk expression. My first paper on Hurston (which I presented at the College English Association conference in 2012 in Richmond, Virginia) featured a statement on her story, "Magnolia Flower," in which I found the use of the river as redemptive. She traveled to write about Haiti, and wrote an important work titled *Tell My Horse: Voodoo and Life in Haiti and Jamaica*.

The target audience includes scholars of African American studies and, in particular, cultural poetics, cultural criticism, folklore, Caribbean studies, and Zora Neale Hurston graduate students, as well as professional researchers and writers. Zora Neale Hurston wrote her most famous work, the novel *Their Eyes Were Watching God*, while in Haiti on a trip funded by a Guggenheim Fellowship, to research the region's transatlantic folk and religious culture for her study, *Tell My Horse: Voodoo and Life in Haiti and Jamaica*. Another work which relates is titled *Haiti and the Americas*, by Carla Calargé (editor), Raphael Dalleo (editor), Luis Duno-Gottberg (editor), and Clevis Headley (editor), publication date, 2013. Haiti has long played an important role in global perception of the Western Hemisphere, but ideas about Haiti often appear paradoxical.

A list of courses in which my book might be used as a text or supplementary text include: African American Literature, Religious Studies, Political Science, Humanities, Digital Humanities, The Study of Archival Research, Caribbean Studies, Haitian Folklore, Zora Neale Hurston, Cultural Studies, Ethnographic Studies, and Rhetorical Study of the Language and Linguistics of Zora Neale Hurston.

My recently published new work with Cambridge Scholars Publishing, *American Women Writers, Poetics, and the Nature of Gender Study*, has a chapter on Zora Neale Hurston's short story, "Black Death," compared to Stephanie Powell Watts's short story, "Unassigned Territory." Author Crystal Parikh contends that "principles articulated as rights in international conventions and treaties—such as the right to self-determination or the right to family—are too often disregarded at home. Human rights concepts instead provide writers of color with a deeply meaningful method for political and moral imagining in their literature of rights made otherwise impossible."[1]

NOTE

1. Crystal Parikh, *Writing Human Rights: The Political Imaginaries of Writers of Color* Minnesota: University of Minnesota Press, 2017.

Chapter Eleven

Reflection on Chapter 4, Nella Larsen

In my lectures, essays, and books, I practice searching for praxis within the study of semiotics. Praxis is the ability of the writer to achieve a high moment of clarity about the human condition. Praxis joins other signs of cultural change, the literary elements of characterization and plot. The writer then creates multiple fields for readers to use and on which to base their visit of the fictional work. The creation of the inner life of a character through narrative lies within the substantive study of the semiotic basis for the narrative by Nella Larsen. Creation of narrative eventually demands characterization and other devices, such as dialogue and dramatic effect, within the creative space in the fictional world. Let us define that creative process and relate to the use of narrative as a semiotic vision. A narrative in the fictional world makes the characters at risk of failure. Larsen uses the humanity of her own experiences as the principle of her fictional works.

Chapter Twelve

Reflection on Chapter 5, Flannery O'Connor

I participated in interdisciplinary theory and practice in the summer of 2017. I endorse and encourage multicultural, historical, linguistic, economic, psychological, philosophical, and sociological insights. My cultural landscape in the research for this chapter involved the different dimensions of Christian spirituality and, in particular, Benedictine spirituality, which I relate to civic values and cultural contexts. I use interdisciplinary and hermeneutical study of traditional resources (historical) and contemporary forms of spiritual life (anthropological). During different difficult periods of my life, my own healing/transformation has occurred and still occurs with readings of Flannery O'Connor. The writing of the project is secondary to the growth that I am receiving. Benedictine virtues of simplicity, listening, obedience, and more come to be the most important aspect. The goals of the project have moved to practicing these virtues.

Likewise, through the peace that I gain by close reading of the collected works of O'Connor and of Thomas Merton, I also perceive them in a new view—that of the twentieth-century modernist sages and peace activists. Through powerful language and poetics, Flannery O'Connor is writing about human rights. I argue that my study of Flannery O'Connor's *A Prayer Journal* indicates the study of the language of trauma. To understand, we compare the passage to the work of Jacques Derrida in "White Mythology." Derrida refers to the depth of metaphor in conceptualization of language. The reversal is such that there can be no final separation between the linguistic metaphorical and philosophical realms.

Chapter Thirteen

Reflection on Chapter 6, Ernest Cline

The creation of the place of dystopian architecture lies within the substantive study of the semiotic basis for the setting by Ernest Cline. His characters move with trepidation within the digital and real worlds. Creation of place eventually demands characterization and other devices such as dialogue and dramatic effect within the dystopian world. Let us define that creative process and relate to the use of both literature and architecture as a semiotic vision. A dysfunctional community in a dystopian world makes the characters at risk of failure. Fear is a predominant theme. Art3mis is a great example of semiotic praxis within the dystopian universe. She represents the space of transformation of the earth itself. One critique writes: "What does Art3mis think of herself? She tells Wade that she's 'Chaotic Neutral' . . . if you're not a Dungeons & Dragons fan, you might not catch the reference. . . . Her whole cure-world-hunger stance is one of the biggest world improvements."[1]

Aesthetic functionality of dystopian structures within the elements of literature builds upon the concept of architecture as a function of a fiction work. Pathos of the dystopian novel relies on dystopian-framed visual context as semiotic praxis. Furthermore, contextualization depends on architecture as an element of the aesthetic creative process. Cline's adventure uses imagined architecture as a lens. Architecture materializes through grammatical structures to create ideologies of social hierarchy. Cline extrapolates to project the future and applies it to an alarmingly unpleasant world. Pedagogical applications of the study of creation of dystopia in *Ready Player One* by Cline explores the work as a creation of an allegory; the work is also a future movie. The dystopian creation works as an opportunity to add significantly to the emotional appeal of the work. Dystopian architecture in the allegory symbolizes representation of place as mythic creation. I approach the pedagogy of the work based on the study of Aristotle's *Poetics* (free online text), a good companion work to interpret "art as imitation." Currently, I am teaching analysis, the writing process, the science-fiction genre, and other key concepts through poetics and hermeneutics, by comparing creation through language. Creation of fiction by my students also supports my framework and acts as a model. We extrapolate about current technology to create science-fiction short stories. Characters live in dystopian spaces which halt human emotions.

Architectural structures materialize post humanity in *Ready Player One* (2011) by Ernest Cline. Through the lens of *Semiotic Praxis* (Mounin, 1985), "Creation of Dystopian Architecture: Semiotic Praxis" investigates dystopian functionality, connectivity, and social order in imagined architecture in the novel. Dystopian functionality in *Ready Player One* finds a basis in the concept of semiotics, the general science of signs, which traces its lineage to Saussure and the American philosopher Charles Sanders Peirce. Jonathan Culler remarks that "Semiotics is an international movement that has sought to incorporate the scientific study of behavior and communication"[2] which clearly embody the methods of Cline in his creation of *Ready Player One*. On page xiv, Mounin fully accepts this differentiation, and the articles in *Semiotic Praxis* manifest a theoretical evolution toward clarifying it. This dichotomy arises from the specific nomenclature generally used by Saussurian semioticians. Central to this nomenclature is the sign which, in strictly Saussurian terms, is defined as an arbitrary relation of a signifier.

Cline uses architecture as a sign. We are studying his use of dystopia through the lens of semiotics. A definition of semiotics reveals the relationship between the architecture that Cline creates with the writing and the vision that Cline wishes to convey. Semiotics studies the life of a sign within society. Mounin writes about art objects, which when viewed, trigger emotional responses. "These responses are indices pertinent to semiotic ion of art interested in semiotic functioning of art."[3] We compare theoretical constructs of Saussurian and Peircean conceptual ideas of semiotics to help the usefulness of both outlooks. My work stimulates a synthesis of theoretical approaches. Saussurian indices are picked up by the observer as possibly leading to knowledge of an aspect of a given natural phenomenon, such as Cline's vision in his concept of the architecture in *Ready Player One*.

Cline sets the book in a social phenomenon where the characters live in the virtual world. The real world is destroyed by the social constructs of the twenty-first century, which embody Cline's psyche and argument in the book. On the other hand, indices are immediate, perceptible facts. Cline uses the contest as a fact to bridge the questions of survival of the inhabitants of earth through architecture and dystopia. Insights into the book *Ready Player One* decidedly use signs to predict drastic cultural change. We become virtual in the book.

With a unique story that combines gaming and internet cultures with that of the 1980s, author Ernest Cline's debut novel uses a space of societal dysfunctionality. His novel reflects our current socioeconomic virtual dependency and is a sign that creates mythic connectivity. The novel, published in 2011, is set in a not-too-distant future where advanced Internet, gaming and virtual reality technologies have changed the world as we know it and led to the creation of the OASIS, a virtual reality universe that people live in and value more than the real world, we experience a "corporate run dystopia."[4] In *Ready Player One,* the author points to a time in the future when unbridled corporate greed creates an alternate condition. Wade, the main character, lives in an old trailer, stacked on top of other rotting trailers. I intend to reveal how Cline uses creation of imagined dystopian architecture to expose that the OASIS ceased to be open-sourced virtual utopia. His vision is a reflection of his interpretation of our current global economic crisis. Cline crafts social order to comment on twenty-first-century greed and economic crisis as well. In addition, a biomimetic look at the book shows loss of the natural world in the genre, as an extrapolation of a darker vision of our future. Cline extrapolates to project an imagined future based on pop culture of the past. He alludes to film, literature, and gaming themes to enhance his work. Ultimately, dystopian creation is important to the meaning of the work. Furthermore, dystopian visions symbolize representation of place. The unity of place and space faces us as a plot device to offer a way to step out of our own universe and into the weird world of the future.

NOTES

1. Evelyn Cook, "Art3mis aka Samantha Evelyn Cook in *Ready Player One*" *Shmoop*, November 11, 2008, Accessed January 10, 2016, http://www.shmoop.com/ready-player-one/art3mis-samantha-cook.html.
2. Jonathan Culler, *Literary theory, a very short introduction* (New York: Oxford, 2000).
3. Georges Mounin, *Semiotic praxis: Studies in pertinence and in the means of expression and communication* (New York: Plenum Press, 1985).
4. Ernest Cline, *Ready Player One* (New York: Random House, 2011).

Chapter Fourteen

Reflection on Chapter 7, Stephanie Powell Watts

Stephanie Powell Watts, associate professor of English at Lehigh University, was one of the ten recipients of a Whiting Award in October 2013 by the Mrs. Giles Whiting Foundation. Watts's debut short story collection (eleven stories) was also a finalist for the PEN/Hemingway Award, the Chautauqua Prize, and the John Gardner Fiction Award. In addition, she has received *The Atlantic* nonfiction prize.

Watts grew up in North Carolina, where many of the stories from her collection are set, and was a Jehovah's Witnesses minister. Watts binds us to ourselves, our memories, and our sense of place. A passionate literary fiction writer, Watts ignites our ability to cope with human suffering, by prayer and respite. In fact, I also bring Jehovah's Witnesses visitors into my home to pray with me. My background as a Judeo-Christian is similar to that of the narrator in "Unassigned Territory." The title of the book places us in the events constructed by the omniscient narrator's language. Her thoughts are paced to show inner life, not only to structure the story, but also to utilize the meaning of words to create action. Language sets into motion the reader's capacity to envision a state of being. The narrator visits a home based on the themes of religious fervor; the narrator learns about herself as a human who needs another human in order to feel. Yet the characters live within the setting, to reveal that place makes us who we are.

In the case of the analysis of the story by Stephanie Powell Watts, I find a shocking reality that begins with the memory of my college roommate. She was a kindhearted, quiet girl who never tried to sway my faith. Now I go back to my experience due to the serious nature of Watts's writing. In the outcome of the reading of "Unassigned Territory," I can reenter my own past experience with a Jehovah's Witness and see that her place in the college was not acceptable to her at all; she had been quite unhappy and in the wrong place. She left college after the semester that we roomed together, a silent and probably suffering Jehovah's Witness who could not use language to share her faith. I also see the capacity to which Watts uses her experiences to write in the same way.

Bibliography

Bostrom, Nick. "Why I Want to Be a Posthuman When I Grow Up." Future of Humanity Institute. Oxford University. (Published in *Medical Enhancement and Posthumanity*, eds. Bert Gordijn and Ruth Chadwick [Springer], 2008: pp. 107–37.

Cather, Willa. *My Mortal Enemy. Project Gutenberg Australia*, Part VII. Accessed October 30, 2018, http://gutenberg.net.au/ebooks05/0500321h.html.

Cline, Ernest. *Ready Player One* (New York: Random House, 2011).

Conner, Marc C. "Modernity and the Homeless, Toni Morrison and the Fictions of Modernism," Part I., *Toni Morison: Memory and Meaning* University of Mississippi Press, 2014.

Cook, Evelyn. "Art3mis aka Samantha Evelyn Cook in *Ready Player One*" *Shmoop*, November 11, 2008, Accessed January 10, 2016, http://www.shmoop.com/ready-player-one/art3mis-samantha-cook.html.

Culler, Jonathan. *Literary theory, a very short introduction* (New York: Oxford, 2000).

DiEdwardo, Joseph. "Unpublished Paper on Nella Larsen". Contributor to *American Women Writers, Poetics, and the Nature of Gender Study,* Ed. Maryann P. DiEdwardo. Cambridge Scholars Publishing, 2016.

Jung, Carl. The Portable Yung. Hull, R.F.C. trans. Edited by Campbell, Joseph. New York: Penguin Books, 1971.

Larsen, Nella. *Quicksand, First Start Publishing eBook,* edition October, 2012.

Mazzoni, Guido. *Theory of the Novel.* Harvard University Press. iBooks. Accessed August1, 2018. https://itunes.apple.com/us/book/theory-of-the-novel/id1190351004?mt=11.

Morgan, Clay. *Undead: Revived, Resuscitated, Reborn* Nashville: Abingdon Press, 2012.

Mounin, George. *Semiotic praxis: Studies in pertinence and in the means of expression and communication* (New York: Plenum Press, 1985).

Peek, Charles A. The Willa Cather Foundation, *Speaking Aloud at Grace Church.* Accessed August 15, 2018. https://www.willacather.org/speaking-aloud-grace-church.

Zauditu-Selassie, K. *African Spiritual Traditions in the Novels of Toni Morrison,* Gainsville: University Press of Florida, 2009.

Index

About the Author

Maryann P. DiEdwardo is the University of Maryland University College UMUC Stanley J. Drazek Teaching Excellence Award (Drazek Award) winner 2017. She is a pioneer of distance learning pedagogy. She teaches English composition and literature for UMUC Maryland University College University College and ESL for VIPKID. She presents lectures on metacognition in the United States and Canada. Her research interests include writing process theory, student-directed learning, fine arts as a paradigm for teaching, and metacognition.

At UMUC, she was a curriculum specialist for The Modern Novel and two classes: 281 and 386. She has been awarded scholarships from Penn State University for her study in theatre arts. An accomplished writer, teacher, author, director, playwright, poet, and motivational speaker, Maryann also teaches research, rhetoric, literature, and active learning. Her fields of expertise include theatre arts and stage history, African American literature, the Romantic Period, drama, poetry, fiction, and nonfiction, as well as creative nonfiction.

She also teaches with social media and Prezi, YouTube, and other modalities, to offer multimodal learning in her classes.

She is an accomplished editor, contributor to journals, and designer of web-based learning. Her methodology of teaching with the learning paradigm, the Socratic method, and the writing process benefits students. DiEdwardo, recipient of two Professional Achievement Awards at University of Maryland University College, also received the 2018 Professional Achievement Award from College English Association. In 2016 she was the recipient of the College English Association's Karen Lentz Madison CEA Award for Scholarship, an annual award for a presentation at the annual conference by an adjunct or contingent faculty member who contributes significantly to the corpus studiorum in English. The prize is funded by an endowment from James R. (Dick) Bennett, and serves to recognize the College English Association's immeasurable gratitude to adjunct and contingent faculty in literature and composition studies, and to honor their unconquerable esprit de corps and professional dedication.

DiEdwardo is known primarily as a landscape painter. Her works are in private collections and galleries. Her en plein air style (literally painting in the open air) compositions evolve from abstract design to integrate design, color, proportions, and balance, and to present poignant images or versions of reality. Recent works include the 36" x 36" oil painting titled "Millbrook Marsh #1 for Joseph Pasda," for the permanent collection at Millbrook Marsh Environmental Center State College, Center County, Pennsylvania, USA; twelve prints presented to New Presbyterian Weill Cornell Hospital, 525 E. 68th Street, New York City: "The Art of Trees" for Child Life Program 2007 and St. Luke's Cancer Center, Bethlehem, PA,

2009; the Pennsylvania State University Lehigh Valley Campus Fogelsville "The Promise of Penn State" Exhibition, January 2008.

Maryann Pasda DiEdwardo was born in Allentown, Pennsylvania, on September 19, 1953. DiEdwardo attended schools in Bethlehem, Pennsylvania, for her primary and secondary education. From 1960 to 1971 she attended private schools to study dramatic art, visual art, and dance. In 1968 she was awarded a scholarship to the Fine Arts Program to study dramatics and art at a summer program for high school students at Westminster College. In 1971 she was elected to Outstanding High School Students of America. DiEdwardo attended the Pennsylvania State University, State College, Pennsylvania, from 1971 to 1975. A summa cum laude graduate and winner of the Carnegie Scholarship, she was graduation marshal for the College of Arts and Architecture, Pennsylvania State University, president of Mortar Board, Phi Beta Kappa, Phi Kappa Phi. While at Penn State, DiEdwardo appeared in major theatrical productions. Her credits include the role of Amelia in *The House of Bernarda Alba*, the reporter from Paris in *The Breasts of Tiresias*, the mermaid in *Ofoti*, and understudy for Joan in *St. Joan*.

Subsequently, DiEdwardo received a scholarship for one year of study at Lehigh University, and eventually earned her master of arts in English from Lehigh University in 1980, with an emphasis on Shakespearean studies. A member of Sigma Tau Delta and instructor in 1976, she also played Ophelia in a production of *Hamlet*, presented for the American Theatre Association in Annapolis, Maryland, that same year.

Maryann Pasda DiEdwardo's professional career in teaching began in 1975 at Northampton Community College. From

1976 to 1979, she served as a professional assistant in the Reading-Writing Lab. In 1977 the Center for Adult Learning chose her as the teacher for Children's Theatre at the community college. DiEdwardo has written, directed, and produced four original musicals with children performing for the public between 1977 and 1979. She was awarded an Outstanding Service Award from Project Aware in 1978. In 2004 she received a doctorate of education from California Coast University. DiEdwardo held positions as adjunct faculty for Lehigh Valley Campus of the Pennsylvania State University, Northampton Community College; adjunct professor for the Department of Arts and Sciences and the Distance Learning Department; as well as adjunct faculty for Lehigh Carbon Community College. She is adjunct professor for Lehigh University.

In 2004, statistical results of case study research suggested that pairing music and linguistic intelligence in the college classroom improves students' grades and abilities to compose thesis statements for research papers in courses that emphasize reading and writing skills (DiEdwardo 2004). In an initial study in 2003, DiEdwardo refined Howard Gardner's (1993) definition of music as a "separate intellectual competence" and compared music intelligence to linguistic intelligence. Furthermore, through acknowledgment of MI theory, educators infuse the cognitive abilities of students by helping them "think," as one of her students suggested. As Howard Gardner suggests: "Very worthwhile. The next step is to figure out why you got the effects that you did. Is music motivational? Does it activate other brain centers? Does it have some kind of intrinsic link to linguistic capacities? Would the effect work the other way around, or with other materials?" (2004 email.) DiEdwardo's case study research connects music as representative of culture and relates to the rhetoric found in literary passages. For example, modern songs with lyrics hold cultural contextual meanings and metaphors such as "A Thousand Miles," by Vanessa Carlton. Students compare songs to current multicultural literature and demonstrate the connections. For example, the work of Chinua Achebe can be understood through the comparison of DiEdwardo's works to the works of modern songwriters. Modern music transforms and allows the student to learn literature, reading, and writing through the theory that promotes transformation.

DiEdwardo currently teaches at Lehigh University and the University of Maryland University College. Film credit: Author of memoir titled *The Legacy of Katharine Hepburn*; interviewed by Bertrand Tessier for a documentary. The French director Bertrand Tessier creates a series of 52-minute documentaries about mythical couples in Hollywood, for French television OCS, a channel dedicated to Hollywood movies. One of the documentaries is about Spencer Tracy and Katherine Hepburn. My book on Katherine Hepburn is a reference. I also have a film credit for my interview with Bertrand, about my book, *The Legacy of Katharine Hepburn: Fine Art as a Way of Life*. It was written in 2004. DiEdwardo's purpose was to revisit an old thesis, the potential historiography of Katharine Hepburn, for educational purposes. DiEdwardo updated the research to include the possibility of a new historiography based on the growing legacy of the famous Katharine Hepburn. Maryann DiEdwardo suggests that "the legacy has just begun to change our cultural views of women and education. I produce activities and goals for educators and families, to use the legacy of this special actress for improvement of lives"

(DiEdwardo, Maryann Pasda, page 79). Her book was published in 2005 and recounts her studies from 1978 to 2005.

CPSIA information can be obtained
at www.ICGtesting.com
Printed in the USA
LVHW091537130619
621125LV00001B/107/P

9 780761 871101